POLITICS AND CIVIL UNREST IN MODERN AMERICA

BY DUCHESS HARRIS, JD, PHD

WITH MARNE VENTURA

Core Library

An Imprint of Abdo Publishing
abdobooks.com

Cover image: Representative Karen Bass spoke about police reform
and the George Floyd Justice in Policing Act on June 25, 2020.

abdobooks.com

Published by Abdo Publishing, a division of ABDO, PO Box 398166, Minneapolis, Minnesota 55439. Copyright © 2021 by Abdo Consulting Group, Inc. International copyrights reserved in all countries. No part of this book may be reproduced in any form without written permission from the publisher. Core Library™ is a trademark and logo of Abdo Publishing.

Printed in the United States of America, North Mankato, Minnesota
102020
012021

 THIS BOOK CONTAINS
RECYCLED MATERIALS

Cover Photo: Alex Wong/Getty Images
Interior Photos: Bill Clark/CQ Roll Call/AP Images, 4–5, 43; Drew Angerer/Getty Images News/Getty Images, 6; Patrick Semansky/AP Images, 8; Red Line Editorial, 11, 21; Hulton Archive/Getty Images, 14–15; AP Images, 19; Julio Cortez/AP Images, 22; Mark Vancleave/Star Tribune/Getty Images, 24–25; Paula Bronstein/AP Images, 26; John Rudoff/Sipa USA/AP Images, 29; Aaron of L.A. Photography/Shutterstock Images, 31, 39; Michael Brochstein/Sipa USA/AP Images, 34–35

Editor: Marie Pearson
Series Designer: Sarah Taplin

Library of Congress Control Number: 2020944170

Publisher's Cataloging-in-Publication Data

Names: Harris, Duchess, author. | Ventura, Marne, author.
Title: Politics and civil unrest in modern America / by Duchess Harris and Marne Ventura
Description: Minneapolis, Minnesota : Abdo Publishing, 2021 | Series: Core library guide to racism in modern America | Includes online resources and index
Identifiers: ISBN 9781532194665 (lib. bdg.) | ISBN 9781644945094 (pbk.) | ISBN 9781098214180 (ebook)
Subjects: LCSH: Politics and culture--Juvenile literature. | Civil rights--United States--History--Juvenile literature. | Protest movements--Juvenile literature. | United States--History--Juvenile literature. | Race relations--Juvenile literature.
Classification: DDC 305.8--dc23

CONTENTS

LAFAYETTE SQUARE

For three days in late May 2020, protests took place across Washington, DC. Many were peaceful. But some people damaged shops and public places. They began looting, or stealing from shops. They started a fire inside a local church. On June 1, DC mayor Muriel Bowser ordered a 7:00 p.m. curfew. The curfew was an attempt to prevent more looting. That evening hundreds of people filled Lafayette Square. The park is north of the

Protesters marched in Washington, DC, in late May 2020. They demanded justice for George Floyd, a Black man killed in police custody.

Military police officers dispersed the crowds in Lafayette Square.

White House. Some people held "Black Lives Matter" signs. They called for an end to racism.

Lines of police officers stood around the protesters. The protesters were mostly peaceful. Half an hour before curfew, the police called for people to leave. In the next few minutes, the police moved in. They threw smoke canisters. The smoke made it hard to see.

Police shot pepper balls. The balls release chemicals that irritate the eyes and lungs. Police hit people with their batons. Most of the protesters ran off to avoid harm. But some threw bricks at officers.

The police cleared the area. Then President Donald Trump walked across Lafayette Square. He went to the steps of Saint John's Church and held up a Bible. Reporters took photos. Then he returned to the White House. The June 1 incident at Lafayette Square sparked controversy. Critics accused Trump of stopping people's

PERSPECTIVES

DEMOCRACY ROLE MODEL?

Journalist Rick Noack wrote an opinion article about the clearing of Lafayette Square. He said people around the world see the United States as a place where protesters are free to speak in public spaces. He argued that the clearing of Lafayette Square had damaged this view. A fence was put up near the White House to keep protesters farther away. He said this might be seen as a sign that the president does not value free speech.

Trump held up a Bible in front of a church for a photo that sparked controversy.

right to free speech for a political photo opportunity. White House officials said the clearing of the park was unrelated to Trump's photo op.

Bowser called the police response unprovoked. Former US Capitol police chief Terrance Gainer said the operation ran against standard training for keeping protests peaceful. Gregory Monahan, the chief of the US Park Police, defended the actions of the police. He said the park was cleared for public safety.

Violent protesters had injured 50 officers during the three days before June 1. New fencing would be put up around the White House to hold back protesters. Neither Attorney General William Barr nor the White House had ordered the officers' use of force.

PROTESTS AND UNREST BEGIN

The US Constitution defends the right to speak freely. Americans have the right to form peaceful groups and ask their leaders for change. Civil unrest happens when people break laws during protests. There is usually disorder or violence. People may damage buildings or cars. They may loot businesses. They may attack police officers or other protesters. Peaceful protest is a right. Civil unrest is a crime.

In 2020 both peaceful protests and civil unrest raged across the country. These actions started on May 25 in Minneapolis, Minnesota. A 46-year-old Black man died in police custody. During an arrest, officer Derek Chauvin knelt on George Floyd's neck for several minutes. Floyd told him that he couldn't breathe. Three other officers with Chauvin did not stop him. Bystanders caught the incident on video. People across the United States watched. Some called for the officers to be charged with murder. Americans protested in every state. They called for an end to racial violence.

DIVISION, PANDEMIC, AND POVERTY

At the time of Floyd's death, tensions were already high in the United States. People were divided in their thinking. Most people were aligned with either the Democratic or Republican party. The two parties disagreed strongly about how best to run the country. This made it difficult for Congress to pass any new laws.

COVID-19 had begun to spread in the United States in January 2020. This disease was caused by a highly contagious virus. By June it had killed more than 100,000 Americans. Black Americans were dying at a higher rate than any other racial group. Many people

COVID-19 AND RACIAL
INEQUALITY

COVID-19 disproportionately affected Black people in many parts of the United States. This graph shows the percentage of Black people in the general population of certain states compared to the percentage of Black people among COVID-19 deaths by April 6, 2020. What do you notice about the graph? How do you think this may have influenced the protests and civil unrest in 2020?

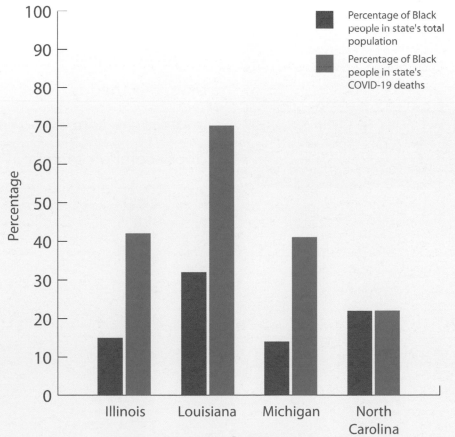

PEACEFUL PROTEST

The US Constitution is the supreme law of the United States. The First Amendment was added to the Constitution in 1791. It gives all Americans the right to five basic freedoms. These are religion, speech, press, petition, and assembly. As long as protesters are not interfering with other people's rights, they have the freedom to assemble. Reporters who attend protests to record the events are also protected under the First Amendment.

lost their jobs due to the pandemic. They were unable to pay for food and housing.

Politicians faced challenges following Floyd's death. They needed to stop the violent behaviors of some. At the same time, they had to address the concerns of peaceful protesters.

STRAIGHT TO THE
SOURCE

After the events of June 1, 2020, two lawsuits were filed against White House officials on behalf of protesters. One lawsuit stated:

This case concerns a day that will live in infamy. It's the day that our federal executive branch unleashed a military and paramilitary force on a band of peaceful protesters assembled in historic Lafayette Park across from the White House. The officials, wielding batons, sprayed the crowd with tear gas, flash-bang grenades, smoke bombs, and rubber bullets, causing frightened protesters to flee, fearing for their lives and hobbled by their injuries. . . . It was a gross abuse of executive power that violated First Amendment free speech rights, Fourth Amendment protections against unreasonable force, Fifth Amendment due process rights, and long-standing federal law prohibiting use of such military force on domestic targets.

Source: Aaron Keller. "Lafayette Park Protesters Sue Trump, Barr, Esper." *Law & Crime*, 11 June 2020, lawandcrime.com. Accessed 15 Sept. 2020.

WHAT'S THE BIG IDEA?
Take a close look at this passage. Why was a lawsuit filed against officials? What details support the complaint? How does the complaint relate to the protesters' rights?

THE ROLE OF POLITICS

There are many examples of racial inequality in modern America. More than 400 years of laws have contributed to this inequality. The slave trade in the United States began in 1619. Enslaved Black people were brought to Jamestown, Virginia. By 1860 nearly 4 million were enslaved in the United States. After the Civil War (1861–1865), the Thirteenth Amendment to the US Constitution ended slavery. But for most formerly enslaved people, the change did not lead to equal rights. In the

A historical illustration shows enslaved Africans arriving in Jamestown. Historical images often included negative stereotypes.

PERSPECTIVES

SEGREGATION

Racial segregation in the South was legal after the end of slavery. Lawmakers passed Jim Crow laws in the late 1870s. These laws forced the separation of people of color and white Americans. The laws were challenged in the US Supreme Court in *Plessy v. Ferguson* in 1896. The court's decision allowed segregation as long as schools and other public places were of equal quality. In 1954 the US Supreme Court changed this ruling. In *Brown v. Board of Education of Topeka*, the court ended segregation in public schools. People who supported segregation said the races were separate but equal. But the Supreme Court said that segregation made schools unequal.

South, schools and public places were segregated. This meant that Black people could not go to the same schools as white people. Unfair rules made it hard for Black people to get good educations, good jobs, or loans. It was hard for them to buy houses. Certain places made Black people pay a tax every time they wanted to vote. Sometimes they had to take tests before voting. The tests were designed to make them fail.

The end of slavery also did not bring an end to violence against Black people. Between 1877 and 1950, more than 4,400 racial lynchings took place. A lynching is the unlawful killing of a person by a mob.

Police brutality against Black people was another problem. A survey in Chicago, Illinois, in the 1920s found that Black people were only 5 percent of the population. But they made up 30 percent of the people killed by police.

CIVIL RIGHTS MOVEMENT

Black leaders organized marches during the 1950s and 1960s. They wanted to gain equal rights for people of color. They wanted an end to racial violence. On March 7, 1965, peaceful protesters gathered on the Edmund Pettus Bridge in Selma, Alabama. They called for voting rights for people of color. Police attacked the protesters with tear gas and clubs. President Lyndon B. Johnson spoke in support of the protests. He signed laws to protect Black voting rights. Still the protests

CIVIL RIGHTS LEADERS

The Student Nonviolent Coordinating Committee (SNCC) was an important organization during the civil rights movement. Two key leaders of the SNCC were Stokely Carmichael and John Lewis. In the late 1960s, Carmichael was a leader for the Black Panther Party (BPP). The BPP helped many people in need. It offered free breakfast programs for children. It helped with health care. Lewis went on to run for Congress. He served from 1987 until his death in 2020.

continued. In July 1967, violence over police brutality broke out in Detroit, Michigan. A total of 43 people died. Hundreds were injured. More than 7,000 were arrested.

In 1968 Johnson formed the Kerner Commission. The group studied the recent unrest. It found that systemic racism was a big cause.

Systemic racism is when systems put people of certain races at a disadvantage. The report said that some police officers, courts, banks, landlords, employers,

Peaceful protesters filled the Edmund Pettus Bridge in Selma, Alabama, on March 7, 1965, as part of the civil rights movement.

and voting officials treated Black people unfairly. The experts advised leaders to change laws that made it hard for Black people to get educations and jobs. They said the government should make programs to help Black people get out of poverty.

CONTINUED DEMAND FOR CHANGE

The civil rights movement brought important legal changes. But the unfair treatment of Black people by police has continued into the 2000s. Black people are more than twice as likely to be shot and killed by police than white people. Yet Black victims are more likely to be unarmed than white victims.

On July 17, 2014, an unarmed Black man died in police custody in New York. Eric Garner called out, "I can't breathe," as officer Daniel Pantaleo held his arm around Garner's neck. Pantaleo had arrested Garner on suspicion of selling cigarettes illegally. Pantaleo was fired five years later. But he was not charged with a crime. Garner's death, like the death of Floyd,

RACIAL ISSUES AND POLICY CHANGES

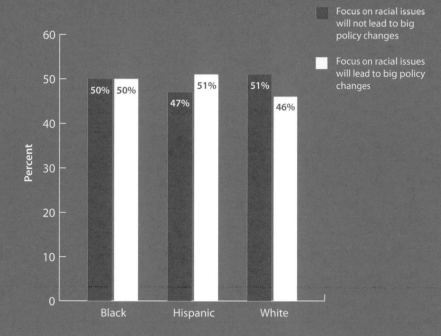

A 2020 Pew Research Center survey asked people if they thought that the increased focus on racial issues would lead to big policy changes that would help address racial inequality. This graph shows how people responded by race. How does this help you understand how people view the influence of public opinion in politics?

followed the use of a police choke hold. This is a move made by police to control someone by holding or pressing on his or her neck. Choke holds are allowed in many police departments when making arrests. Activists

Some police departments require officers to wear body cameras. The cameras record what happens when the officers respond to calls.

called for police choke holds to be banned. Experts on police behavior say this and other reforms might help end unnecessary force. For example, departments could keep better records on the use of force by police. They could provide more training for officers. They could require police to wear and use body cameras.

The Black Lives Matter (BLM) movement is one force working for change. The BLM Foundation's mission is to stop white supremacy. This is the belief that white people are better than people of other races. The BLM Foundation works to stop the violent treatment of Black people by police and by racists. Its goal is to improve the lives of Black Americans. When the video of Floyd's death became public in May 2020, more people joined BLM. Black Americans were joined by protesters of every race around the world.

EXPLORE ONLINE

Chapter Two talks about segregation and laws that treated Black people unfairly after the Civil War. The video at the website below goes into more depth on this topic. How is the information from the website the same as the information in Chapter Two? What new information did you learn from the website?

JIM CROW
abdocorelibrary.com/politics-and-civil-unrest

BACKLASH ACROSS AMERICA

Following Floyd's death in Minneapolis, protests there continued for several days. There were riots. Some people damaged buildings, looted, and set fires. More than $500 million worth of property was damaged in the city. State officials sent in Minnesota National Guard troops to control the violence. More than 430 people were arrested over two nights.

Meanwhile, people held protests around the country. In Portland, Oregon, protests began peacefully on May 29. The crowd

The civil unrest following George Floyd's death included looting and fires.

Trump sent federal officers to Portland in response to the protests.

marched down a city street. People chanted "Black lives matter" and "No justice, no peace." But the event turned violent. Some of the marchers started breaking shop windows and spray-painting shops. Some shot guns and set fires. Mayor Ted Wheeler declared a state of emergency. He ordered a curfew for the city.

Police used flash-bangs and tear gas to disperse the crowds. Oregon governor Kate Brown called in the National Guard. The Mark O. Hatfield Federal Courthouse was the center of the protests. Some protesters smashed windows. They tried to light fires at the courthouse doors. In response Trump sent federal officers to Portland in early July. Some officers wore camouflaged uniforms. They forcefully removed protesters from the streets and put them in unmarked vans. Protesters thought they were being kidnapped. Troops used flash-bangs and pepper balls to disperse protesters. The number of protesters had been dropping since the end of May. But they rose to more than 1,000 that weekend.

The handling of Portland's civil unrest led to political conflict. Portland leaders said that most protesters were peaceful. Only a small group of people were causing trouble. Local leaders did not want Trump to send in federal officers. Brown said Trump didn't care about public safety. Trump said Portland leaders had lost control of the city.

A group of mothers in Portland began protecting protesters. They formed a human chain around the crowd. It became known as the Wall of Moms. They stood together to face the federal officers and

BOOGALOO BOIS AND PROUD BOYS

Some groups have incited violence or added to the violence during the riots. Those groups include the Boogaloo Bois and the Proud Boys. The Boogaloo Bois is a group of mostly white men. They support gun rights and the overthrow of the government. They often wear Hawaiian shirts and carry weapons at protests. In June 2020, a man with ties to this group was charged with murdering an officer during BLM protests. Proud Boys is an all-male group. It opposes BLM. The Southern Poverty Law Center calls it a hate group. In September 2020, three men believed to be linked to Proud Boys were sued. They were accused of shooting at people and committing other violent acts.

show support for BLM. They were joined by a Wall of Dads. They used leaf blowers to blow away tear gas shot by police. A group of military veterans joined as well.

In Seattle, Washington, protesters took over an area of the city in early June. After a week of conflict, the Seattle Police Department abandoned the area. It let protesters stay without police presence. Protesters gave

The Wall of Moms protesters marched through Portland in support of BLM.

speeches, read poems, and made music. They showed films about the criminal justice system. City officials hoped that allowing this would improve relations between protesters and police. Trump criticized local leaders for not controlling the unrest. As time went on, several shootings happened in the area. There were reports of sexual assaults. The city and police took back the area on July 1.

By the first week of July, there had been more than 4,700 protests around the country. People in 2,500 US cities had joined marches. An estimated 15 million to 26 million people participated. In comparison, the civil rights marches in the 1960s involved hundreds of thousands of people. BLM may be the largest protest movement in US history.

The BLM movement aims to end police brutality and other issues of systemic racism.

REASONS FOR PROTEST

Experts suggested several reasons why so many people joined the movement. One is that social media and the news have made information easy to find. People can quickly learn about Black people's deaths in police custody. Celebrities have posted support for the BLM movement. NASCAR driver Bubba Wallace had "Black Lives Matter" painted on his race car. He drove the car in a June 10, 2020, race.

Another explanation is that laws and the treatment of Black people are still not equal. The Kerner Commission released its report in 1968. A 2018 study found that conditions for Black people had not improved. A larger percentage of Black people were unemployed than in 1968. The median white family had ten times more wealth than the median Black family. Black families still faced issues getting home loans. Black business owners were less likely to get business loans. Segregation was illegal. But systemic racism still kept schools and neighborhoods segregated. Many Black children were still not getting good educations.

Protesters turned out for a variety of reasons. They demanded fair treatment for Black people and other people of color. They demanded change.

EXPLORE ONLINE

Chapter Three explores some of the reasons for protest following the death of George Floyd. What is one of the main points of this chapter? What evidence is included to support this point? Read the article at the website below. Does the information on the website support the main point of the chapter? Does the website present new evidence?

PROTESTERS CALL FOR JUSTICE

abdocorelibrary.com/politics-and-civil-unrest

POLICY CHANGES

Politicians responded to the protests. On June 17, 2020, Republican senator Tim Scott proposed a police reform bill. The bill encouraged bans on choke holds. Scott's bill raised the penalties for false police reports. It offered federal grant money to police departments that used body cameras. It called for a database of police who break rules. It made lynching a federal crime. It required more de-escalation training for officers. This training would help them handle

Senator Tim Scott introduced his police reform bill in June 2020.

BLACK PEOPLE IN GOVERNMENT

Historically, Americans have elected few Black people into government positions. The number is rising today. But more work is needed. The Congressional Black Caucus is helping. Its members belong to Congress. They work to make sure that people of color have the same opportunities in government as white people.

more situations without using force.

The bill needed the approval of 60 of the 100 Senators. On June 24, Senate Democrats voted against Scott's bill, and it did not pass. They criticized it for being too weak. They called for a change to qualified immunity for police. That was not in Scott's bill. Qualified immunity is a privilege that keeps government officials from being sued for actions taken in the line of duty. Many officers who have shot and killed people could not be sued.

On June 25, 2020, the US House of Representatives passed the George Floyd Justice in Policing Act. It was written by several Democrats. If made law, this act would have banned choke holds and racial profiling. Racial profiling happens when police have a bias about certain races. Because of those biases, they target people of certain races as suspects. Officers may use race as a reason for stopping someone. Black drivers are often pulled over by police even though they haven't broken any laws.

The act would have ended qualified immunity. It would have moved money from police departments to community programs that help those in need. In order to become a law, the act needed to pass the Senate as well as the House. The Senate was controlled by Republicans. They disagreed with Democrats about what policies would work best. This meant the act was unlikely to pass in the near future.

Congress may not have quickly passed new laws. But state and local leaders made some quick changes. New York State ended the practice of keeping secret the records of police who abused people. Philadelphia, Pennsylvania, and more than 20 other cities banned choke holds. Many leaders at the state level spoke out. They said a national standard for police would help regulate the use of force by officers.

CONTINUED DEMAND FOR CHANGE

Peaceful protests brought some change. But civil unrest continued. On August 23, 2020, an event sparked further protests. Police were called to a home in Kenosha, Wisconsin. The caller said a man named Jacob Blake would not leave her property. Officers learned that Blake had a warrant out for third-degree assault,

Some people set fire to businesses in Kenosha, Wisconsin, after the shooting of Blake.

charges that Blake later pleaded not guilty to, and tried to arrest him. He resisted. They tased him, but it didn't work. He walked away and leaned into the front seat of his car. One officer shot Blake several times in the back. Witnesses caught the shooting on video. Investigators found a knife in Blake's car. It was unclear whether Blake was holding the knife when he was shot. Blake survived the shooting. But he faced the possibility of being unable to use his legs.

Protesters marched in Kenosha after Blake's shooting. They called for police reform. Protests during the day were mostly peaceful. At night some people destroyed property. On August 25, a small group of men with guns showed up after being asked by a Kenosha business owner to help protect his properties. Among the group was 17-year-old Kyle Rittenhouse. During a confrontation, Rittenhouse shot and killed a protester. He shot two others while fleeing, killing one and injuring another. Rittenhouse's attorney said his client was acting in self-defense.

On August 29, BLM protesters and Trump supporters confronted one another in Portland, Oregon. Trump supporter Aaron Danielson died from a gunshot wound to the chest. Police suspected an antifa supporter named Michael Forest Reinoehl shot him. Police tried to arrest Reinoehl. But the man pulled out a gun. Officers shot and killed him.

Politics and civil unrest were brought to the center of attention after the death of George Floyd. While protesters call for an end to systemic racism, it is up to politicians and local governments to restore peace and pass laws that protect all people.

STRAIGHT TO THE
SOURCE

The National Association for the Advancement of Colored People promotes equal rights for people of color. It wrote in favor of the George Floyd Justice in Policing Act. The statement read:

> The legislation represents unprecedented action and a significant first step to prevent and address violence against the Black community by law enforcement all over the country.
>
> While there is more to be done, the legislation seeks to hold law enforcement officials accountable for their actions. . . .
>
> We now call upon the Senate to put partisanship aside and do the right thing by passing this [influential] legislation. The Black community and, indeed, our entire nation cannot afford to risk one more life and wait for one more day.
>
> Source: "NAACP Applauds House Passage of 'George Floyd Act.'" *NAACP*, 26 June 2020, naacp.org. Accessed 2 Sept. 2020.

CONSIDER YOUR AUDIENCE

Adapt this passage for a different audience, such as your younger friends. Write a blog post conveying this information for the new audience. How does your post differ from the original text and why?

IMPORTANT DATES

1791
The First Amendment is added to the US Constitution, giving people the right to protest peacefully.

1865
The Thirteenth Amendment ends slavery.

March 7, 1965
Peaceful protesters in Selma, Alabama, call for equal voting rights for people of color. Police attack them.

July 17, 2014
Eric Garner dies in police custody in New York City.

May 2020
George Floyd dies in police custody in Minneapolis, Minnesota, on May 25. People hold protests in the city for several days afterward.

June 2020

On June 1, police clear protesters from Lafayette Square in Washington, DC. Later in the month, Seattle, Washington, police abandon an area of the city as protesters take over. On June 17, Republican senator Tim Scott proposes a police reform bill. It is not signed into law. On June 25, the House of Representatives passes the George Floyd Justice in Policing Act. It is also not signed into law.

August 2020

Jacob Blake is shot during a police arrest on August 23. On August 25, Kyle Rittenhouse is accused of killing two and wounding one during a protest. On August 29, Trump supporter Aaron Danielson dies after being shot by Michael Forest Reinoehl during a clash between protesters in Portland, Oregon.

STOP AND THINK

Surprise Me

Chapter Two discusses the history of racism and police brutality in the United States. After reading this book, what two or three facts about this history did you find most surprising? Write a few sentences about each fact. Why did you find each fact surprising?

Dig Deeper

After reading this book, what questions do you still have about politics and civil unrest? With an adult's help, find a few reliable sources that can help you answer your questions. Write a paragraph about what you learned.

You Are There

This book discusses the George Floyd Justice in Policing Act. Imagine you are a representative or senator in Congress. What act would you write to make life better for Americans? List at least five ideas in your proposal. Be sure to add plenty of detail.

GLOSSARY

brutality
the act of being cruel and heavy-handed

curfew
a rule made by government leaders that orders all people off the streets at a given time

disperse
to cause to scatter or break up

flash-bang
a device that creates a loud noise and a blinding light when thrown

pandemic
an outbreak of a disease that infects a relatively large percentage of people around the world

pepper ball
a bullet-like device shot from a gun; it releases a chemical that hurts the eyes, nose, and lungs of its target

poverty
the state of being poor, or not having enough money to meet basic needs

racism
the belief that people of certain races are inferior

riot
the act of a group causing violence and disorder in public places

tear gas
a gas that irritates people's eyes

ONLINE RESOURCES

To learn more about politics and civil unrest in modern America, visit our free resource websites below.

Visit **abdocorelibrary.com** or scan this QR code for free Common Core resources for teachers and students, including vetted activities, multimedia, and booklinks, for deeper subject comprehension.

Visit **abdobooklinks.com** or scan this QR code for free additional online weblinks for further learning. These links are routinely monitored and updated to provide the most current information available.

LEARN MORE

Bjornlund, Lydia. *Modern Political Parties*. Abdo Publishing, 2017.

Harris, Duchess. *Black Lives Matter*. Abdo Publishing, 2018.

ABOUT THE AUTHORS

Duchess Harris, JD, PhD

Dr. Harris is a professor of American Studies and Political Science at Macalester College and curator of the Duchess Harris Collection of ABDO books. She is also the coauthor of the collection, which features popular titles such as *Hidden Human Computers: The Black Women of NASA* and series including Freedom's Promise and Race and American Law. In addition, Dr. Harris hosts the *Freedom's Promise* podcast with her son.

Before working with ABDO, Dr. Harris authored several other books on the topics of race, culture, and American history. She served as an associate editor for *Litigation News*, the American Bar Association Section of Litigation's quarterly flagship publication, and was the first editor in chief of *Law Raza*, an interactive online journal covering race and the law, published at William Mitchell College of Law. She has earned a BA in History from the University of Pennsylvania, a PhD in American Studies from the University of Minnesota, and a JD from William Mitchell College of Law.

Marne Ventura

Marne Ventura has written over a hundred books for kids. A former elementary school teacher, she holds a master's degree in education from the University of California. Her favorite topics include history, science, arts, crafts, and food. Marne and her husband live in California.

INDEX